C000138293

IMAGES OF ENGLAND

KING'S HEATH HIGH STREET
HIGH STREET
A NOSTALGIC JOURNEY

IMAGES OF ENGLAND

KING'S HEATH HIGH STREET
A NOSTALGIC JOURNEY

BOB BLACKHAM AND ANDY BISHOP

TEMPUS

This book is dedicated to the memory of Stan Budd, a keen local historian who devoted his long life to the collection of archive material, photographs and memories concerning King's Heath and generously shared them with fellow enthusiasts.

We would like to thank Mrs Molly Budd for permission to use many of the photographs in this book and the members of King's Heath Local History Society for their help and encouragement in the production of this book.

First published 2007

Tempus Publishing
Cirencester Road, Chalford,
Stroud, Gloucestershire, GL6 8PE
www.tempus-publishing.com

Tempus Publishing is an imprint of NPI Media Group

© Bob Blackham and Andy Bishop, 2007

The right of Bob Blackham and Andy Bishop to be
identified as the Authors of this work has been asserted in
accordance with the Copyrights, Designs and Patents Act 1988.

All rights reserved. No part of this book may be reprinted
or reproduced or utilised in any form or by any electronic,
mechanical or other means, now known or hereafter invented,
including photocopying and recording, or in any information
storage or retrieval system, without the permission in writing
from the Publishers.

British Library Cataloguing in Publication Data.
A catalogue record for this book is available from the British Library.

ISBN 978 0 7524 4481 9

Typesetting and origination by NPI Media Group
Printed in Great Britain

Contents

Acknowledgements

We would like to thank the following for allowing us to use their photographs in this publication:

Molly Budd
King's Heath Local History Society Archive
King's Heath Library Digital Photograph Archive
Birmingham Museum and Art Gallery
Andy Bishop
Bob Blackham
Beverley Boden
Boots Archive
King's Heath and Moseley Baptist church
Kathleen Cottrell
Gary Lanham
Alf and Janet Russell
Barrie Geens

Every effort has been made to acknowledge the owners of original photographs shown within this publication.

Introduction

The Early History of King's Heath by Ivor Davies

This book is mainly about King's Heath High Street, but also includes that section of Alcester Road South that contains part of the central shopping area. It is on the High Street that today's King's Heath began and, in order to appreciate why and how, some historical details are necessary.

Little is known of the area before the late eighteenth century. A few earlier references mention land adjacent to it but tell us nothing about King's Heath itself. However, in the eighteenth century, it would certainly still have been entirely rural and sparsely populated, with a number of farms and the dwellings, probably mostly isolated, of those who worked on the land. A large expanse of common and heath stretched across the later High Street and Alcester Road South. There was no village or hamlet.

After the Norman Conquest, Kings Norton, Moseley and King's Heath were all in the Royal Manor and Parish of Bromsgrove, hence the name, the King's Heath. By the thirteenth century, Kings Norton had become a separate royal manor and a virtually independent parish, although owing nominal allegiance to Bromsgrove church. Only in 1846 was the link finally severed.

In 1564, Queen Elizabeth sold the Manor of Bromsgrove but kept Kings Norton as a royal manor and parish, which included King's Heath as part of the Moseley Yield, one of four divisions for tax purposes. Moseley was a village long before King's Heath began to grow but there has always been a close relationship between them, so that, even today, it is difficult to say where one ends and the other begins.

King's Heath is between three and four miles from Birmingham and this proximity ultimately decided its long-term future. More immediately, it was one of the causes of its growth from the late eighteenth century onwards.

A trackway ran across the heath which gave Worcestershire farmers access to Birmingham markets. It is said that eighty packhorses daily carried produce from Evesham to Birmingham in the eighteenth century and cattle and sheep would also have been driven along the road. Birmingham's population began to rise in the second half of the century, resulting in an increasing demand for food. This would have brought more traffic across the heath.

It would have been hard going on the road, particularly in winter, as little maintenance was likely to have been carried out. Manors were gradually losing their authority, so in 1555 Queen Mary established the parish as the unit of local government. The church vestry was to be responsible for certain secular duties, one of which was the upkeep of the parochial roads. This depended on forced, unpaid labour, so the task was unlikely to have been done well on a regular basis.

Already, during the 'turnpike mania' of 1751-72, which finally created a dense network of turnpike roads, an Act of Parliament passed in 1767 had put the road from Spernal Ash to Digbeth, via the King's Heath, in the care of a turnpike trust who were to maintain and improve the highway. The cost was met by charging tolls to traffic and gates were set up at intervals for this purpose. It is doubtful that turnpiking the road had more than a marginal effect on the increase in traffic, though it did eventually make the journey easier. The main cause, however, was Birmingham's burgeoning population, which expanded enormously in the hundred years that followed, from about 70,000 in 1801 to 522,000 in 1901.

Improvement to the road seems to have been slow. In 1781 it was criticised as being too narrow but it was only in the early nineteenth century that the road was straightened and its surface made more durable. By 1840 it was said to be 'improving'.

The increasing traffic helped to promote development along the road on both sides of the present High Street. The first inn, the Cross Guns, dates from the late eighteenth century. It was made by converting two cottages in 1792, according to a sign displayed on the front of the building. A pear tree growing outside predated the conversion and gave the pub its local name. A much bigger building replaced it in 1897. The Hare and Hounds followed between 1824 and 1828, while the King's Arms at Alcester Lanes End was formed by joining a cottage and a shop in the late 1790s.

There is no definite record of which other services were available before 1841 but it is reasonable to assume that there would have been a smithy early on and, perhaps, a wheelwright. There may also have been a few shops, particularly in view of an event which took place a few years after the turnpiking of the road.

In 1772, an Act was passed for dividing and enclosing the commons and wastelands within the Manor and Parish of Kings Norton in the County of Worcester. The award of 1774 benefited the larger landowners most and resulted in the formation of a number of fairly big estates on which substantial houses were later built, probably in the period of 1790-1820. Additional farmland was also brought into use.

The changes – namely, the growth of Birmingham, improvements to the road and the enclosures – must have led to an increase in jobs in the area – for example, servants and estate workers for the big houses – and a demand for facilities to satisfy the needs of the increasing population.

Unfortunately, no plan of the 1774 awards is extant and the first firm record we have of the physical development of King's Heath is the map of 1840 made in connection with the 1836 Tithe Commutation Act, which abolished tithes in kind and substituted a money payment.

This map shows the presence of a small village along the present High Street and some buildings on two side roads – Silver Street and Poplar Road. There is a farm on the turnpike road, approximately on what is now the Sainsbury's site, with a few cottages opposite. A number of big houses are also shown, two of them, the Grange and Kingsfield, adjacent to the road, with driveways leading to them. There is little else before Alcester Lanes End and King's Heath is still a predominantly rural community.

However, the map shows another feature which gave further impetus to growth. In 1840, the Birmingham and Gloucester Railway passed through King's Heath and a station – called Moseley until 1867 – was opened there. By this time, Birmingham was less than half an hour's train ride away and this easy access to the town helped to promote the more rapid expansion of King's Heath in the second half of the nineteenth century.

It is easy to trace the changes on the ground in the next forty years or so if we compare the 1840 map with the first edition 25ins Ordnance Survey Map of 1884. Most of the High Street is now built up, together with Silver Street and Poplar Road. There are new roads – Valentine, Middleton and Albert. Development has begun to move out from the High Street with house building on Vicarage and Avenue Roads and along the turnpike road beyond Wheelers Lane towards Alcester Lanes End.

It is easy to see the physical growth of King's Heath from this map but it is harder to appreciate the changes in lifestyle which went with the expansion on the ground. Most people who lived in the King's Heath of 1840 were still engaged in agriculture or small handicrafts, or else providing for the basic needs of those who were. By 1884, this was no longer true.

Fortunately, some record of the changes is provided in the trade directories which become available at this time. *Bentley's History, Gazetteer, Directory and Statistics of Worcestershire* in 1841 gives the first mention of King's Heath in its Kings Norton section. It lists the names of some local inhabitants as well as their occupations.

Between them, they cover the range of basic necessities for a small community which is beginning to grow. There are two grocers and a baker; two boot and shoe makers; a blacksmith and a mason; a grocer/farmer/butcher and a farmer/cooper; two beer sellers and three victuallers; a fire-iron maker; a police officer and a railway official; a rope spinner and a manufacturing chemist – who must surely have plied their trades elsewhere – and a number of farmers.

Over the next forty years or so, services increase greatly in both number and variety. A count of entries in the commercial sections of various directories gives some indication of the speed of change. The 1854 *Post Office Directory* has only eighteen entries in a separate King's Heath list with farmers still being included in Kings Norton. In 1856 there are thirty-nine; in 1868 – forty-six; in 1871 – sixty-one; the 1880 (now *Kelly's*) *Directory* gives eighty-eight; while 1884 has one hundred and twelve.

Besides giving the number and variety of services, directories also tell us approximately when they first became available. A chemist, for example, is listed in 1867 and a doctor in 1883. Earlier entries show provision chiefly for everyday needs like food and clothing but the later ones point to a changing lifestyle. In 1868, two haberdashers, a dressmaker and a tailor are included; in 1871, a newsagent; in 1876, a laundry; in 1878, a bookseller; 1882 has two gas fitters and a piano tuner, while in 1884 a house decorator, sewing machine agent and two coffee houses are all listed. Surprisingly, perhaps, a sub-post office first appears as early as 1858.

As previously noted, Birmingham was growing rapidly in the nineteenth century and great pressure on housing led to expansion into the countryside. During its own growth, King's Heath managed to avoid the worst aspects of Birmingham's development – the squalid back-to-backs, defective sanitation and polluted water. It came to be known as a healthy spot in which to live and, even before being formally annexed to the city, was, by the end of the century, well on the way to becoming a dormitory suburb where people could live and travel into town to work.

It developed uniform rows of terraces with larger houses for the better-off. In 1871, there were 410 houses and a population of nearly 2,000. By 1891, both figures had more than doubled to 940 and 4,610. In 1901, the population was 10,078.

During the last decade of the nineteenth century, estates at each end of the High Street were taken over for housing. Addison, Drayton and Goldsmith Roads were built on land from the Alcester Road Estate (Kingsfield) in 1890, while at the bottom of King's Heath, the Birmingham Freehold Land Society purchased the Grange Estate in 1895 and seven new roads were laid out. As farming decreased in importance, the inhabitants became a mixture of business, industrial and professional middle class, together with artisans, many of whom worked in Birmingham.

Meanwhile, necessary changes had taken place to fit King's Heath for its new role. Various institutions suitable for a town or, as it turned out, a suburb were in place by 1900. Pubs have already been mentioned and, in the nineteenth century, churches were also established. The Baptists were first with a church in 1815, rebuilt in 1872 and 1898, on its present site in the High Street. All Saints church followed in 1860 and was given its own parish in 1863, while in 1887 a Methodist church was erected in Cambridge Road. There was also a corrugated-iron Catholic church in Station Road in 1896.

Law and order were not neglected either. The first police station was built on the corner of the future York Road, next to the Hare and Hounds, in the 1850s and later removed to Balaclava Road. From 1852, the Magistrates' Court sat in a room upstairs at the Cross Guns. In 1893, a new police station and court house were built on a site near the railway.

There was a brewery, dating from 1831, behind the Cross Guns, where the licensees brewed their own beer, but it barely outlasted the century before being sold off to Birmingham Breweries and closed.

After the 1870 Education Act, local boards were set up to build and run state schools in areas without adequate voluntary provision. The first such school in King's Heath was erected in 1878 at the corner of the future Institute Road. This was not the first school in King's Heath however. A schoolroom, connected with Moseley Church School, had been located at the site of the later All Saints church in 1856 but closed due to lack of finance in 1876.

On the corner opposite the Board School, the King's Heath and Moseley Institute was opened in 1879. This was a middle-class venture in entertainment and education. The Institute arranged lectures, plays and musical shows. Evening classes were held at a small private school opened to prepare fee-paying pupils for grammar school. It had a library, reading room, coffee room and gym. A workingmen's club occupied the basement. There were facilities for private parties, dances and meetings of local organisations, of which there were a considerable number at this time.

A horse omnibus from Birmingham to King's Heath was operating in 1851 but services were infrequent and interrupted. Although buses were still certainly running to Alcester Lanes End as late as 1885, the advent of the trams probably killed them off. A steam-tram service to and from town began in 1887. The route terminated at All Saints church and there was a depot in Silver Street. A short distance further along that street a volunteer fire brigade started in 1886. Whilst on the High Street, the London and Midland Bank opened an imposing building in 1898.

As most of the changes already described were in or around the High Street, it seems surprising that it is not quite clear when the name was officially adopted for that part of the Alcester Road between Queensbridge and Vicarage Road. It first appears in a single entry of *Kelly's Directory* for 1888. By 1895 it is in general use in the listings. However, locally it was probably current well before the first date. Previous directories assigned relevant entries to Alcester Road. 'South' was added to the latter in the early 1920s to distinguish it from Moseley's road of the same name.

Other changes beyond the control of anyone in King's Heath ultimately settled the future of the town. A Local Government Act of 1894 created civil parishes with elected councils; Kings Norton became a Rural District Council, of which King's Heath was a ward returning two councillors.

Just four years later, the civil parishes of Kings Norton, Northfield and Beoley were amalgamated as the Kings Norton and Northfield Urban District Council with greater powers than the parish councils. By this time, Moseley and King's Heath were the most populous part of the new authority and there was some local agitation for independence – but to no avail. Little more than a decade later, the Urban District was absorbed by Birmingham.

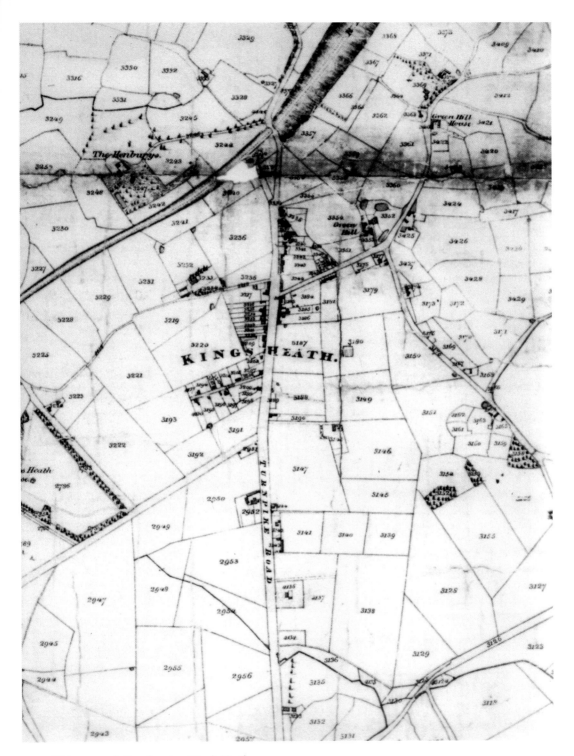

Tithe map of 1840 showing King's Heath.

King's Heath in the Twentieth and Twenty-First Centuries
by Margaret Shepherd

King's Heath at the turn of the twentieth century was still a rural community, despite the growth in population during the latter part of the nineteenth century. Most of the roads leading off the main Alcester to Birmingham road were still country lanes. The population was mixed with a few wealthy families like the Cartlands and others 'living on their own means' and able to employ one or two servants. There were professional people, but the number of poor families was large. Accounts from various churches show how they tried to help these people, particularly during severe winters and at Christmas. Concerned about the number of hungry children in school, the Kings Norton and Northfield District Council which managed King's Heath before it was part of Birmingham set up feeding centres. The one in King's Heath was in the parish hall, where breakfast was served every day at a nominal charge. It consisted of bread with dripping, porridge and cocoa. Later, the church extended the scheme to include dinners and some of the better-off boys in school subscribed to help the poorer ones.

In 1902 an application was made to Andrew Carnegie, the Scottish millionaire, for money to build a free library. A subscription list was opened to buy a piece of land on the Grange Estate between Station Road and the police station. The foundation stone was laid in 1905 and the library opened in 1906. Next door was the Seventh Day Adventist church and three shops. In the early 1920s the church became Hope Chapel. The congregation remained there for fifty years before moving to larger premises in Moseley. The building was demolished and an extension to the library built which is now the children's section.

In 1907 transport to Birmingham improved with the demise of the steam tram, a mode of transport mourned by no one as the trams had been slow, dirty and noisy. The new electric trams extended the route passing the old depot in Silver Street and finishing at Alcester Lanes End.

By 1908 the district council faced a severe problem with schooling as the original school on the High Street was full. Thus a new school was built in Colmore Road and opened in 1911. In November of the same year, King's Heath became part of Birmingham.

A new form of entertainment came to the village in 1912 with the opening of King's Heath cinema in Institute Road, and later a second opened in York Road at the back of the Hare and Hounds. This was later wired for sound and closed in 1932.

In 1915 Colmore Road School became a military hospital and the children were moved to King's Heath where part-time schooling continued until 1919. In 1923 a plaque was put up in All Saints church to commemorate the men of King's Heath who had died in the war and a Calvary was erected in the churchyard. The British Legion based in Station Road hold their yearly service of remembrance there.

During the early 1920s, most of the farms and farmland disappeared as Birmingham City Council built new estates at Billesley, Warstock, Pineapple and Dad's Lane to house slum clearance from the city centre and King's Heath became more of a city suburb than a rural village. In 1926 the Outer Circle bus route was completed. This was dubbed 'the bus which went nowhere' as it covered a twenty-six-mile circular route linking the outer suburbs. Many paid a shilling to go all the way round, passing through parts of the city they had never seen before during the two-and-a-half-hour ride. This bus, along with the trams and the train, made King's Heath a popular shopping centre. The shops were varied, with a large number of grocers, bakers, butchers and greengrocers, the largest of which was Cooper's opposite the church. There were also stationers, jewellers, ironmongers and drapers but two shops that did good business during the Depression of the late twenties were the pawn brokers in York Road and Poplar Road. By the early thirties, entertainment had changed with the opening of the Kingsway Cinema on the Parade – a row of shops which replaced cottages. The earlier buildings had long front gardens which became an access road and later a car park. In 1932 the Institute closed and Woolworth's acquired the site, opening its store there in 1934. Home entertainment was looming, too, as could be seen with the opening of wireless and record shops.

In March 1939 King's Heath School closed and staff and pupils transferred to new premises in Wheelers Lane. The old building was used during the war by Masons the grocers as a storage depot. King's Heath was bombed between August 1940 and April 1941 and, during this time, over a hundred civilians were killed. The railway station was closed in 1942 and the site sold for retail. In 1945 Masons moved out of the school building. However it became needed as a school again and was not finally closed until 1982 when a new building was opened on Valentine Road. The old school was demolished and shops built on the site.

In 1948 the closed churchyard next to the parish church was transformed when the gravestones were laid flat. Eight years later in 1956 the Victorian vicarage was demolished and St Dunstan's Roman Catholic church built to replace the one bombed in 1941. It was consecrated in 1968.

By the 1960s the character of King's Heath had changed again. In 1952 the trams ceased to run and there were buses only to the city centre. By this time, however, private cars were becoming more numerous and congestion on the High Street was growing steadily. A bypass or a bridge has been considered but rejected. The advent of television saw the demise of the Kingsway, which became a bingo hall, and the dog track at Alcester Lanes End which became a housing estate. Another link with the past went in 1962 with the demolition of the old parish hall next to the church and the building of a new one beyond the church car park. The arrival of the supermarket saw the closing of the individual food shops; their premises have since become estate agents, charity shops and restaurants with just one butcher, one baker, one greengrocer and two chemists surviving.

Now, in the twenty-first century, there are further changes planned. The vicarage has been demolished and the site is to be used for community purposes beginning with a medical centre, optician and chemist to be followed later by facilities for the elderly and a village square.

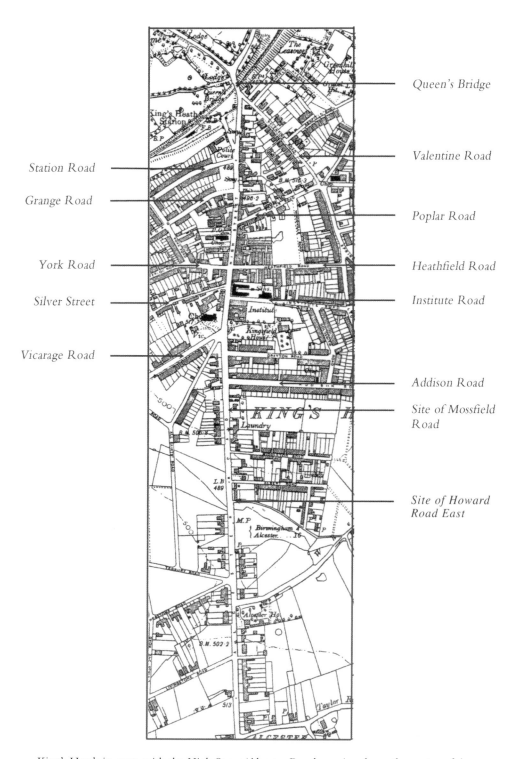

Station Road

Grange Road

York Road

Silver Street

Vicarage Road

Queen's Bridge

Valentine Road

Poplar Road

Heathfield Road

Institute Road

Addison Road

Site of Mossfield Road

Site of Howard Road East

King's Heath in 1903, with the High Street/Alcester Road running down the centre of the map.

King's Heath High Street: A Nostalgic Journey

Howard Road East to Vicarage Road

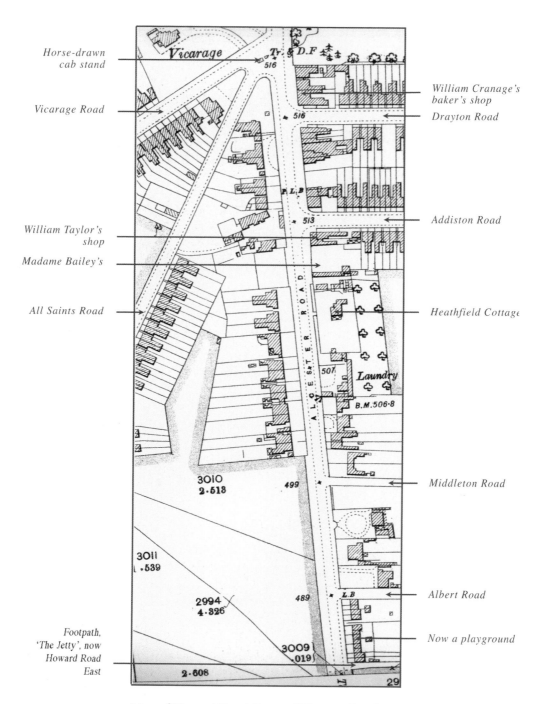

Horse-drawn cab stand

Vicarage Road

William Taylor's shop

Madame Bailey's

All Saints Road

Footpath, 'The Jetty', now Howard Road East

William Cranage's baker's shop

Drayton Road

Addiston Road

Heathfield Cottage

Middleton Road

Albert Road

Now a playground

Map of Howard Road East and Vicarage Road.

Above and below: Our journey towards Birmingham along the Alcester Road and High Street of King's Heath begins at the junction with Howard Road. The picture above from the 1920s shows that Howard Road East had not yet been constructed. The row of old terraced houses stood at the busy road junction where there is now a children's playground (see below). A small footpath ran along the side of the end house towards Wheelers Lane long before Howard Road East was constructed. It was known locally as 'the Jetty'. It is still there today and is an ancient footpath.

Above: The picture above shows the end cottage after the construction of Howard Road East in 1931. This row of old houses was knocked down in the 1970s. The path known as the Jetty can clearly be seen heading towards Wheelers Lane.

Below: This postcard shows a view of the opposite side of the Alcester Road at the junction with Howard Road. The view faces towards the centre of King's Heath. These more modern semi-detached and detached houses contrast with the old terraced houses facing them.

ALCESTER RD. SOUTH   KINGS HEATH

Above and below: These two views are taken from the same spot looking from the end of Mossfield Road towards Addison Road. They were taken about 100 years apart. The photo below shows the old Safeway store, in the centre right, which is now the LA Fitness Centre. Neither of the modern blocks of shops is featured in the older photograph; the beautiful shaped hedges and small white fence belonged to Heathfield Cottage.

Heathfield Cottage was reputedly built in the late 1790s. By 1838 it was occupied by Moss Todd. He was the owner of the Kings Arms pub. He died at the house on 18 May 1848. His wife Diana and then his son Joseph Moss Todd lived there until the 1870s. By the early 1900s the house was owned by George Hardy who ran the Waterloo Bar at the top of New Street in Birmingham.

Eventually, a road was cut along the side of the cottage to join the Alcester Road and this was named Mossfield Road after Moss Todd. The house then became No. 69 Alcester Road until it was knocked down in 1964. If you look into Mossfield Road today all that remains of the house and grounds is a huge old beech tree in the LA Fitness Centre car park.

The two photographs on this page show the shops that run from Mossfield Road to Addison Road. The photograph above shows Madame Bailey's millinery shop. It was first recorded in King's Heath around 1920 and remained in business until the 1980s.

By 1965 Safeway had built its first shop in King's Heath on the site of Heathfield Cottage next door to Madame Bailey. Safeway remained there until the 1980s when they moved to a site opposite King's Heath Baptist church.

Left: Madame Bailey's shop. This picture was taken in the 1990s and yet the shop had a timeless quality. The picture could easily have been taken in the 1950s or even earlier. The shop itself retained the delicate stained-glass decoration above its large front window. Even outside the shop, there remained a well-worn section of the old paved surface when the rest of the pavement surrounding had been replaced by modern slabs.

Below: Mr Parkes Pantry on the corner of Addison Road in the 1980s: a very popular baker's and cooked-meat shop at the time.

This old postcard shows William Taylor's drapery store at the corner of Addison Road in the early 1900s. His shop was there from 1914 until the 1960s. The other shops heading towards Mossfield Road were: John Potter (dairyman), Poole's (ladies' outfitters), Miss Campbell (milliner), Arthur Bach (confectioner) and Madame Bailey (milliner). Directly opposite the end of Addison Road was Church Farm. It was kept by Henry Chinn from the 1840s.

These two modern postcards show the shops on either side of the Alcester Road, from Addison Road to Drayton Road, in the late 1960s. All of the buildings in these two views are still very recognisable today even if the traders are different. Sydney Brown's furniture shop, above left, became a branch of the TSB in the 1980s and is now the Pear Tree public house.

This picture shows the first Sainsbury's store at the far end of the row of shops on the right. Sainsbury's was the first shop in the row to be built; it opened in 1966. In 1974 Sainsbury's built a larger store with a multi-storey car park next door to its original one. The old shop was occupied first by Lloyds Bank and currently by Lloyds TSB.

The picture above shows the TSB between Drayton Road and Addison Road in the 1980s. They originally occupied the building next to the Kingsway Cinema (now the Gala Bingo Hall) opposite the end of Grange Road. They moved to the site near the corner with Drayton Road in the 1980s.

Wetherspoon's pub the Pear Tree took over the old TSB building in 2003.

The view looking south along the Alcester Road with the corner of Drayton Road visible on the left.

A view of the junction of Vicarage Road, Alcester Road and All Saints Road. In 1887 steam trams first came to King's Heath. Their journey from Birmingham went as far as Silver Street where the tram depot was situated: anyone needing to venture further south would have had to take a horse-drawn cab from the stand at the corner of Vicarage Road. The cabs were run by Alfred Sheppard and his sons from 1874. Sheppard had previously been the landlord of the Hare and Hounds from 1866-74.

This corner view of the Alcester Road and Drayton Road shows William Cranage's bakers at No. 19 Alcester Road. They opened in 1907.

The same shop can be seen at the far right of the following postcard from the 1920s. By then it was Charles Weare's bakers shop. The shop next door was King & Son's drapers shop at No. 15. This view is looking from Drayton Road towards Institute Road.

This picture shows a later view of the same row of shops from Drayton Road. The baker's shop eventually became a branch of the National and Provincial Bank. It is now the Nationwide.

The same shops are pictured here. This photograph shows how King & Son had expanded to become 'Kings: The House for Value'. Next door was D.B. Flowerdew's fishmongers shop. Then there was Arthur Jones' decorating shop. His sign advertises: 'Glass, lead, oils, colours and paperhangings'. This shop eventually became York Supply in the 1960s.

This picture shows the same shops again and an early motor car following a tram along the Alcester Road.

This photograph shows the Hedges Buildings. They are named after Hedge's Pharmacy, shown in the centre. To the right is Thomas Twigg's stationery shop. It is recorded in King's Heath from 1913. By the 1970s it was Twigg's newsagents shop. It finally closed in the 1990s. Frank Farrand's shop was a grocer's shop. Amy Adams began selling children's clothes from her terraced house in King's Heath in 1933. The site of her first shop was on the corner of Kingsfield Road, which she took over in 1934. Adams is still there today.

Vicarage Road to Institute Road

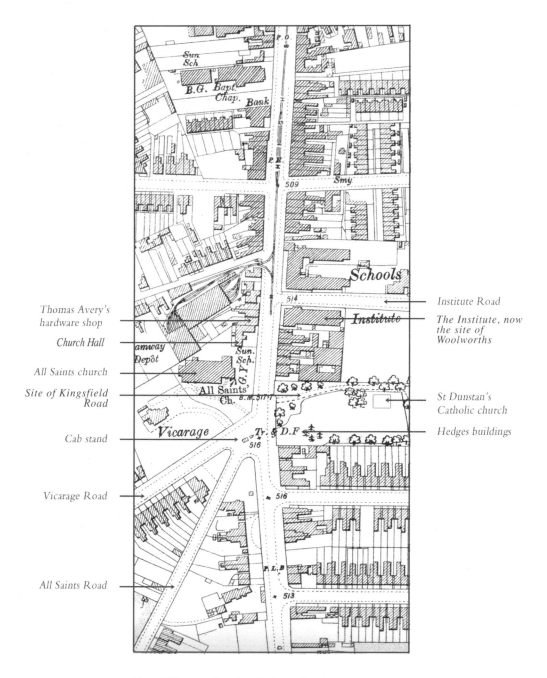

Thomas Avery's hardware shop

Church Hall

All Saints church

Site of Kingsfield Road

Cab stand

Vicarage Road

All Saints Road

Institute Road

The Institute, now the site of Woolworths

St Dunstan's Catholic church

Hedges buildings

Map of Vicarage Road to Institute Road.

These two postcards show the same view, but a closer inspection reveals a large area of trees present in the earlier picture next to Hedges Buildings.

In this picture, they have been replaced by a modern brick-built group of shops. The trees and small wooden fence mark the entrance drive to the grounds of Kingsfield House. The house is now gone, but is remembered in the name of the small road that was built following its driveway: Kingsfield Road.

Kingsfield House is first mentioned in 1826 when it was purchased by Charles Dean, a whitesmith. Joseph Henry Nettlefold bought the house and lived there from 1871 until his death in Pitlochry, Scotland in 1881. Alban Gardner Buller then acquired the house. He was a solicitor, JP, and county councillor for King's Heath. He lived there from 1886 until 1924. Just before his death he sold the house, its apple and pear orchards and grounds to the Roman Catholic Church. St Dunstan's High School was established in the house in April 1924.

The house was also used as a temporary place of worship after the original St Dunstan's church was destroyed by a German bomb on Good Friday 1941. The house was eventually demolished in 1953.

Above and below: These two views show the modern structure of the new St Dunstan's Roman Catholic church. The current church was built in 1968 in front of the old church building – just visible in the picture – built in February 1953. This is now used as the church hall and was built on the lawn in front of the site of Kingsfield House. The schools behind were built in the gardens and orchard. Bishop Challoner School was built in 1953 and St Dunstan's Primary School in 1964.

On this page are two of the most common views on a King's Heath postcard. All Saints church was built in 1860. The building just visible to the right of the church was the old Sunday school building, built before the church in the 1850s. It was later used as the original church hall.

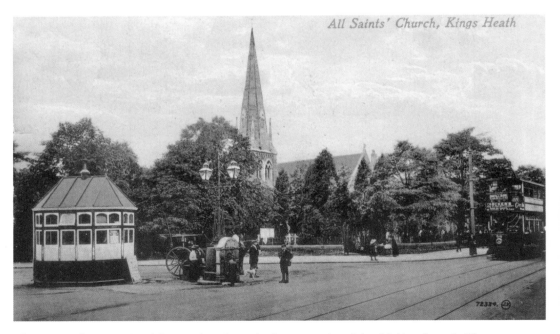

The corner of Vicarage Road features the cab stand, a horse trough and the drinking fountain. The fountain was built to commemorate Queen Victoria's diamond jubilee in 1897.

Above and right: These two photographs show the demolition of the original vicarage of All Saints church in 1955. It had been built in 1870 at a cost of £275 and had fifteen rooms. However, by 1955 plans had been drawn up to replace the old building with a more modern vicarage.

Above: Half of the old vicarage was demolished whilst the vicar continued to live in the other half of the building.

Left: The new vicarage was then built on the site of the original one.

Opposite above: The new vicarage was completed in 1956. However, it only stood for fifty-one years. In early 2007 the garden was cleared and the second vicarage of All Saints church was also demolished.

Opposite below: This photograph was taken when the house was empty, just a few days before it was demolished.

Above and below: These two photographs taken in the 1960s show the old Sunday school building that stood on the High Street next to All Saints church. By this time it was being used as the church hall. It was demolished soon after and a new church hall was built next to the vicarage. Bon Marché now occupies this site.

A view of the High Street looking towards Institute Road on the right. The wall of All Saints church is visible to the left. The building with the tall tower was King's Heath Board School. The postcard also shows two old small steam trams passing one another in the distance.

This postcard shows a later view featuring an electric tram. The tram line was electrified and extended to Alcester Lanes End in 1907.

High Street, Kings Heath

This view shows an early motor car parked by the kerb and flanked by various horse-drawn vehicles.

Opposite above: Another similar view with Institute Road on the right. The shop on the far right of the picture is Cooper's greengrocers at 161 High Street. They arrived in 1913. Next door is Walwyn's shoe shop. Then there are: Charles Thompson's chemists, David K. Baxter's drapers, Emily Robinson's confectionery shop and finally J.W. Pearsall's butchers shop at 153 High Street.

Opposite below: This picture dates from some time after 1949 when buses replaced the tram service. Timpson's shoe shop is now occupying the shop next to Cooper's.

This picture sees a group of men, deep in conversation, huddled under the awning of Emily J. Robinson's confectionery shop at 155 High Street. Robinson's is listed there from 1915 until the 1960s.

This view shows a wonderful row of glass lights hanging outside Cooper's and Thompson's shops on the right. A Union Jack flag is also flying amidst the trees.

This postcard shows the King's Heath and Moseley Institute and King's Heath Board School on the corner of Institute Road on the right. The Board School is the building with the tall tower and the Institute has iron railings outside.

This picture shows the King's Heath and Moseley Institute looking south along the High Street.

The King's Heath and Moseley Institute was built in 1878 on the corner of the High Street and Institute Road – the site of Benjamin Sawyer's old cottage. He was the foreman at the old brick yard upon which the Board School was built. The first public subscription list reached nearly £750. Joseph Henry Nettlefold donated £200, Mr John Cartland gave £100 and Isaac Bate, owner of the Cross Guns, donated £50. Only the rooms fronting the High Street were built in the original phase. The large

lecture hall, with its fine stage, was erected at the rear along Institute Road in 1882. The two different phases are evident in this picture and the one on the previous page.

The Institute was originally built because many residents had expressed a desire to establish a public news and reading room for the village. It was, for many years, the focal point of the local community, hosting concerts, dances, lectures, dramatic performances and many other social activities. However, by the late 1930s attendances had dropped and the building was leased to F.W. Woolworth & Co. in 1933. They eventually knocked the old building down in the 1970s.

This picture dates from 1968 and shows part of the new Woolworth's store already built alongside the Institute. The Institute was knocked down and the new store extended to the corner of Institute Road.

Above: These two fabulous photographs show the interior of Woolworth's store in King's Heath. The counter pictured above is selling sandwiches, bournvita, cakes, pastries, Horlicks, fresh milk and coffee.

Below: This counter is advertising 'suitable Christmas gifts' and has an old cash register on the top.

Above: The picture above was taken at a special black tie ball inside the main hall of the Institute in the 1920s.

Below: Woolworth's new store was finally completed in 1974 and all traces of the Institute disappeared from King's Heath except the name, Institute Road.

Above and below: These two postcards show the row of shops opposite Woolworth's looking towards Silver Street. A steam tram (above) has just left the Silver Street depot. The shops at the far left were built next to the old church hall (where Bon Marché stands) and were as follows: Thomas Avery's ironmongers, C.H. Greaves' grocers, Ault's men's outfitters, Chapman & Sanders' stationers (see page 50), Cecil Cariss and Kellett, auctioneers, and Joseph Herbert's coffee house.

Above and left: Chapman & Sanders was a well-known local stationery shop on King's Heath High Street opposite Woolworth's. It was owned and run by two ladies, Jessie Chapman and Edith Sanders. They set up their shop in the early 1900s. They were apparently concerned what effect the arrival of Woolworth's in 1933 would have on their business. However, the shop remained in business until the 1950s.

A busy High Street with Institute Road on the right and Silver Street on the left. The notice on the departing tram reads: 'Alcester Lane to Hill Street.'

This picture shows a later view with Woolworth's occupying the ground floor of the old Institute building on the right, whilst the Board School appears to be missing the top of its tower. The entrance to the old tram depot on the corner of Silver Street on the left has been replaced by the modern Midlands Electricity Board showroom building. The building on the other corner of Silver Street was Joseph Henry Skan's tobacconists shop which opened in 1910.

Institute Road to Heathfield Road

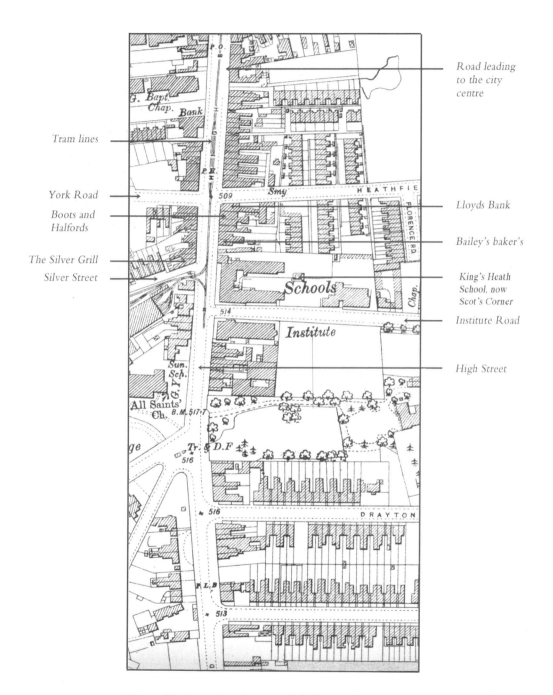

Road leading to the city centre

Tram lines

York Road

Boots and Halfords

The Silver Grill

Silver Street

Lloyds Bank

Bailey's baker's

King's Heath School, now Scot's Corner

Institute Road

High Street

Map of Institute Road to Heathfield Road.

Above and below: These pictures were taken in 1982 and show the old Board School building, on the corner of the High Street (above) and along Institute Road (below), boarded up ready for demolition. The school opened on 12 August 1878. The attendance was seventy-six boys, seventy-four girls and sixty-four infants. It was built on the site of an old brick yard well known in the area.

Above and below: These two pictures show the construction and completion of the Scot's Corner development which now stands on the site of the old Board School building. Shops within the new development include McDonald's, Clark's shoe shop and Thornton's sweet shop.

Above: The well-known restaurant and snack bar, the Silver Grill, occupied the old site of Skan's tobacconists shop on the corner of the High Street and Silver Street in the 1970s and '80s.

Below: In the 1990s, the Silver Grill finally closed and the AA took over the site. Today it is an Acorns charity shop.

George Rowley Bailey's bakery and cake shop was situated opposite the end of Silver Street at 151 High Street next door to the Board School building. He set up business in King's Heath in 1909 although the shop front says, rather ambitiously, that it was established in 1777. It may have been, but sadly elsewhere and definitely not in King's Heath. His shop eventually closed in the 1950s. It is now the site of Johnstan's butchers shop.

Bread
Cakes
Pies . .

QUALITY
ALWAYS
FIRST.

THE SHOP
THE CHILDREN
LIKE.

Of every description imaginable, baked in the latest and healthiest manner. Veal and Ham, and Pork Pies made fresh every day—the Pies with the delicious seasoning, that are just different from any others in the Town.   TRY ONE TO-DAY.

G. R. BAILEY,

151, High St., *The Café*, King's Heath

Above: An advert for Bailey's bakery, or 'The Café'.

Below: Lloyds Bank in the 1970s occupying the building on the corner of Heathfield Road. They moved there in 1915.

Boots arrived in King's Heath in 1912 and was originally situated at 129 High Street opposite the Midland Bank. On 7 January 1932 it moved to 147 High Street, as shown in the picture. Next door at 145 was Joseph H. Tay's butchers and 149 was the Maypole Dairy Co. In June 1967 the shop was knocked down and replaced by the larger store that still trades today at 145-147 High Street.

Heathfield Road to Poplar Road

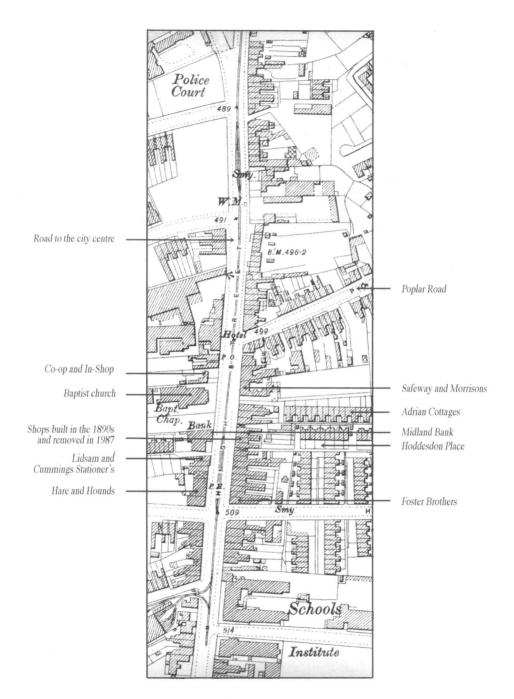

Map of Heathfield Road to Poplar Road.

This postcard shows the High Street from the early 1900s with the old Hare and Hounds on the far left.

The postcard above shows a very evocative picture of King's Heath with the Hare and Hounds on the corner of York Road some time in the 1920s. Next to the pub is the entrance to the Ideal Cinema. Opposite is Mr Hague's drapery on the corner of Heathfield Road with Foster Brothers next door. Foster's opened in 1905 and Hague's in 1909.

Opposite above: This very early photograph of King's Heath High Street features the old Hare and Hounds. Standing outside is Levi Cottrell who became tenant landlord in 1879. Levi knew the owner of the pub, Isaac Bate, as he had worked as groom at his King's Heath residence, the Grange.

Opposite below: It was noted that there were only three oil lamps to light King's Heath in the early 1800s: one at the Cross Guns, one in the butcher's shop (where Somerfield now stands) and one above the Hare and Hounds. This photo shows that a street lamp has replaced the old oil lamp. This group photograph was taken after 1897 when Edward Collins, who married Isaac Bate's widow Eleanor, owned the pub. The man with the apron is possibly Edward Collins, but more probably his bar manager George Skidmore.

These two remarkable photographs show the gardens behind the Hare and Hounds in the 1880s. The man leaning on the bench in this picture is landlord Levi Cottrell. Behind him are the summer arbours under which his customers could sit whilst enjoying their drinks.

This view is looking at the rear of the Hare and Hounds. The family are stood on the lawn which, in 1852, is described as the 'quoit ground', where games of quoits were played.

This picture shows just how small the original Hare and Hounds pub was. The pub is the building with the bay windows and portico. The plain doorway to the left of the bay window was the entrance to the tap room. The building to the left of pub, on the corner of York Road, was an entirely separate structure. Built after the pub, it was originally used as the town's first police station until the 1850s. It contained three cells measuring 8ft by 10ft.

A view of the front of the building. From the 1870s to the 1890s it was the private residence of Samuel Whitehouse. From 1896-1901 George Bladon ran his dairy business from here. It was demolished with the old pub in 1907.

Right and below: The new Hare and Hounds was built in 1907. It replaced the old inn built between 1824 and 1828 by Aaron Payton. The Hare and Hounds has a long association with law and order in King's Heath. Part of the old inn was the town's first police station and it stood on the corner of York Road. The landlord at the time, Aaron Payton, was an early constable in King's Heath before a proper police force was set up. In fact, the stocks and whipping post were sited on the opposite side of the High Street to Milford Place. The new Hare and Hounds pub is a Grade II Listed Building due to it retaining its Art Nouveau tiles in the corridor by the York Road entrance as well as other features of importance.

KING'S HEATH, BIRMINGHAM.

This view looking south, with Heathfield Road on the left and York Road on the right, shows the huge entrance to the Midland Bank on the far right. The next big building is Lindsay and Cummings' stationers and library on the corner of Milford Place. Further up is Thomas Thompson's boot shop and then the old Hare and Hounds.

KING'S HEATH.
NEAR BIRMINGHAM.
"SCOTT" SERIES.   NO. 379

Opposite was a beautiful row of buildings. The shops at either end of this stretch of the High Street had very ornate gables and sandwiched between was a plainer block of shops; sadly, these buildings were pulled down in 1987.

HIGH ST KING'S HEATH

This picture shows, on the left, Neale's Tea Stores (with the sign on the first floor) and, on the right, the new Hare and Hounds, Lindsay and Cummings' stationers and Eastmans' butchers.

Opposite above: An architect's plan for the row of seven shops that ran from the corner of Heathfield Road. They were planned in December 1890 for John Collins who was listed as living in King's Heath.

Opposite below: A busy, sunny scene at a spot just outside the Hare and Hounds, with the Midland Bank visible to the left. The people seem rather relaxed as they stroll across the road, as does the photographer. Crossing the High Street at the same point today, one might encounter rather more traffic.

This later view shows Halfords' shop next to A.C. Clarke's tobacconists on the left. The right side shows Spier's furniture shop next door to the Hare and Hounds.

Opposite: Barr's pork butchers was at 125 High Street opposite Milford Place from the early 1900s. Butchers would often display their meat outside like this. It must have been some feat to hang the animals on the top row, however. Mr Barr is third from the left.

Left and below: Miss Cecilia Ellen Comely's fancy repository and library was at 135 High Street (next to Foster Brothers' shop) from 1910 to the 1930s. She then moved to opposite the Kingsway Cinema. Her shop and Lindsay and Cummings' stationers, on the opposite side of the High Street, called themselves 'libraries'. Comely's had needlework and fancy goods at the front of the shop. The 'library' was a small room at the rear of the shop.

Comely's Library
HIGH STREET,
KING'S HEATH.

READ AND BE WISE.

The loss of the above section of shops from Heathfield Road to present-day Somerfield in the 1980s lost not only ornate architecture but two old King's Heath place names. The small alley that now leads to Somerfield's car park originally led to a row of sixteen houses called Adrian Cottages.

Further up the High Street, opposite Milford Place, was another alley called Hoddesdon Place. This led behind the shops where there was another row of thirteen houses. All are sadly now gone.

Above and left: These two photographs are of the frontages of shops taken in 1985. Second City Seconds was at No. 109 High Street, whilst the Country Garden was at No. 127.

A detail of the third floor of the shops that would today be nearest Somerfield. They were Nos 109–113. The detail clearly shows the construction date of 1896.

Shops at the other end nearest Heathfield Road, being prepared for demolition.

Left: Foster Brothers' shop was trading in King's Heath from 1905 until the 1990s. Its original shop was the one just before the corner. However, by the 1960s it had expanded to occupy 137 and 139 High Street. Eventually in the 1970s it occupied only the corner shop.

Below: By 1986 plans were afoot to demolish the row of shops and replace them with plainer, more modern-looking shops. This picture shows the start of the process as the scaffolding was erected around the shops ready to begin demolition.

Above: Construction of the new shops in 1987.

Below: When the new shops were complete, Fosters reoccupied their corner position for a few years. However, they eventually ceased to exist as a business and another clothes shop took their place on the High Street. This ended Fosters' association with King's Heath, which had lasted for nearly 100 years.

Above: Where Somerfield now stands was the site of a tiny cottage, dwarfed in the picture above by its much taller neighbours. From the late 1700s onwards King's Heath High Street was made up of many cottages like these, but they were all gradually replaced in the late 1800s and early 1900s.

Below: The old cottage was Thomas Knowles' butchers/hucksters shop in the 1770s. By 1875 it was being run by Charles Elton who also ran the post office next door. In 1891 he left to run the Cross Guns and William Bluck, pictured here, took over the shop until the 1920s.

Above: Another view of the construction of the new shops looking back towards Heathfield Road.

Below: Safeway moved from their original site near Mossfield Road in the 1980s. They took over the existing Presto supermarket, which had been built on the site of the old butcher's shop and post office. In more recent years the shop has been occupied by Morrisons and it is currently Somerfield.

Above: This unusual view of the Baptist church and the Midland Bank was taken after the shops on the corner of Heathfield Road were demolished in 1987.

Left: The very ornate Midland Bank (now HSBC) building dates from 1898. However, this replaced an earlier London and Midland Bank building that stood on the same site in the 1880s. It was a much smaller building set back from the High Street with bay windows and a front yard. It had a garden to the rear for the bank manager and his family, who lived above the bank.

Above: Opposite Somerfield stands King's Heath Baptist church. The present church (shown here) was opened on 4 May 1898. This is the third chapel to be erected on this site.

Baptists were first recorded in King's Heath during the Priestley Riots of 1791 when the house of William Piddock was burned down. His house was inhabited by a blind Baptist called John Harwood. William Piddock owned a piece of land on Poplar Road where Somerfield car park now stands. His house was on this site.

Right: A small wooden cottage was first built for worship on the site of the present church in 1815. This was replaced by a new stone chapel (pictured here) in 1872.

Left: Matthew Court's drapers shop, pictured above in the 1890s, was an old building situated next to the Baptist church where In-Shops now stands. His wife Matilda and daughter Dorothy are pictured in the doorway.

Below: Court's old shop was demolished and replaced by the TASCOS (Ten Acres and Stirchley Co-operative Society) department store in the 1930s. The photograph shown here was taken in 1986 when the old TASCOS building was occupied by the Co-op Seasons shop which was closing down. This building burned down in July 2001 and has been replaced by the new In-Shops building.

Poplar Road to Station Road

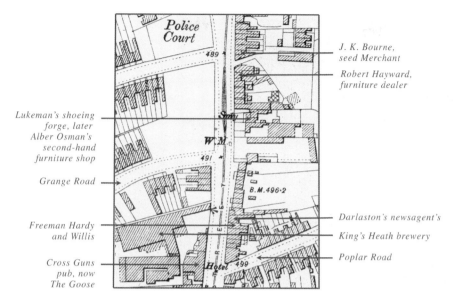

J. K. Bourne,
seed Merchant

Robert Hayward,
furniture dealer

Lukeman's shoeing
forge, later
Alber Osman's
second-hand
furniture shop

Grange Road

Freeman Hardy
and Willis

Cross Guns
pub, now
The Goose

Darlaston's newsagent's

King's Heath brewery

Poplar Road

Above: Poplar Road to Station Road,
earlier map.

Below: Poplar Road to Station Road, later
map.

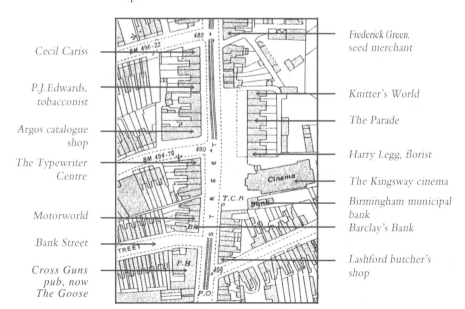

Cecil Cariss

P. J. Edwards,
tobacconist

Argos catalogue
shop

The Typewriter
Centre

Motorworld

Bank Street

Cross Guns
pub, now
The Goose

Frederick Green,
seed merchant

Knitter's World

The Parade

Harry Legg, florist

The Kingsway cinema

Birmingham municipal
bank
Barclay's Bank

Lashford butcher's
shop

This watercolour shows the original Cross Guns Inn. It was created in 1792 by knocking through the dividing walls of two old cottages that faced onto the High Street. Locals called the pub 'the Pear Tree' as it had a very large Jargonelle pear tree growing across its front. By the 1840s the pub was being run by James and Sophia Bate. The last cottage on the far right was separate from the pub. It was a shop run by Phoebe Davis. The old shop was demolished in 1878.

Opposite: These pictures show the corner of Poplar Road. It was originally called Adams Lane after Charles Adams, a wheelwright who lived on the road. A toll gate was erected across the High Street and another across the end of Poplar Road in the late 1700s. This was to prevent people trying to pass into Poplar Road on their way towards town without paying the toll. The building with the curved corner wall was Lashford's butchers shop for many years from 1913 onwards. It is now Heritage Estate Agents.

The last landlord of the old pub was Charles Elton. His name can be seen above the door in this picture. The old pub was demolished in 1896.

Opposite: The new Cross Guns pub was built in two separate phases. The main part of the pub, the right-hand section, with three ground-floor bay windows, was built in 1897. Originally situated at the far end was the stable block. This was replaced in 1898 when a new smoke room and first-floor billiard room were added. The landlord at the time was Charles Elton. He died at the pub during the works in October 1898. He is buried in All Saints churchyard. He was a founder member of King's Heath volunteer fire brigade, formed in 1886, and also a Freemason.

The Cross Guns pub during the late 1980s. In 1996 the Cross Guns was boarded up and refurbished. Its black and white timbers were repainted in a more colourful livery.

After more than 200 years it was decided to change the pub's name and it reopened in 1997 as the Goose and Granite. This name did not last quite so long and it is currently called the Goose, as pictured here.

King's Heath Brewery was the first and biggest industry in King's Heath. It stood directly behind the Cross Guns and its area covered the whole of Bank Street. It was originally set up in the mid-1800s by the Bate family who also ran the Cross Guns pub. From the 1860s it was called Isaac Bate & Co. In 1878 it was bought by Frederick Everitt who in turn sold it to Birmingham Breweries in 1896. It closed in 1902 and was demolished in 1904.

Isaac Bate and his wife, Eleanor, pictured outside their house, the Grange. Isaac died at the house in June 1885. The house was demolished in 1896 and Grange Road built across it.

The Typewriter Centres finally left King's Heath in the 1990s. However, the shop is still involved with communication of a more modern kind as is it is now a mobile-phone shop. Pride's dry cleaners and Sweeney's radio and television shop had been on the High Street since the 1960s.

Opposite above: The row of shops from Bank Street to Grange Road. Featured here is the old Barclays Bank building that gave Bank Street its name. It was originally the United Counties Bank in the early 1900s and Barclays in the 1930s. By the 1990s it had become a betting shop.

Opposite below: The Motor World shop at No. 62 High Street was the site of another TASCOS shop. It was set up in the 1930s as a grocer's. It replaced Walter Mynor's ladies' outfitters, which had been there since 1905. Next door was Cowen's jewellers shop.

A 1915 photograph showing the shops that ran from the corner of Poplar Road down the High Street opposite Bank Street. Here we can see Edgar Jarrett's watchmakers and jewellers at No. 83 and John Bradbury's ironmongers at No. 79 High Street. Further down on the right amongst the trees, set back from the road, the old George Inn once stood. This beerhouse dates back to the 1860s. It was set up by

Charles Payton, nephew of Aaron Payton who founded the Hare and Hounds. It finally closed in April 1903 when its license was refused due to convictions for allowing drunkenness and illegal gambling.

Above: The following two pictures were taken from the same spot about ninety years apart. This one shows the row of shops and old cottages that ran from Poplar Road all the way down to opposite Station Road, including James Lester's butchers at No. 73 and Walter Cowen's plumbers (the advert on his wall states 'only first-class men employed'). The two shops nearest us, encroaching onto the pavement, were Walter's fish and fruit store at No. 69 and (closest of the two) Henry Edwards' china dealers at No. 65 High Street. Most of the old shops and cottages were eventually knocked down in the 1930s and a new row was built set back from the roadside. This new row was called 'the Parade'.

Below: This photograph shows the same view, but the row of new shops set back from the road called the Parade has replaced the older shops and cottages.

Above: The photograph above shows Albert Osman's second-hand furniture shop at No. 47 High Street. He is first listed there in 1903. He took over the premises of what was Charles Lukeman's shoeing forge. The original blacksmith's forge building is the small structure to the left of the house.

Below: Row of shops opposite Station Road. The figure on the pavement is standing at the entrance to the yard of Lukeman's shoeing forge and later Albert Osman's shop. Cash Converter's shop occupied the site until March 2007.

The shop at the far end by the Kingsway Cinema was Harry Leggs the florist. It is now Blockbuster DVD rental shop.

The Parade under construction in the 1930s. Only two shops were occupied at the time and the 'Cariss' sign covering the windows shows that they were dealing with letting the shops. The shop at the end on the left was Powell's florists shop.

The Parade with all the new shops occupied. Next to Leggs was The Chocolate Shop, then a cycle shop with rows of bicycles displayed outside. The Donald Allen photographic studio was the next shop, with the Birmingham Royal Institution for the Blind next door; then came Edna Teece's ladies' hairdressers shop.

Above: This picture, taken in the 1990s, shows how some of the shops were later knocked through to make much bigger shops such as the massive Knitters' World shop.

Left: The building next to the old Kingsway in the 1990s. It was originally a branch of the Birmingham Municipal Bank from the 1920s until the 1970s. It then became the Trustee Savings Bank (until they moved to the shop which is now the new Pear Tree pub). Bradford & Bingley, the building society, then took over this building. Today it is Electronix Clearance Corner, a shop that sells electrical goods.

Essoldo Bingo Hall in the 1980s. The building was originally the Kingsway Cinema which was built in 1924 and finally closed in 1980. It is currently the Gala Bingo Hall.

A photograph taken in 1987, showing the Argos catalogue shop which arrived in King's Heath in the 1970s.

This photograph dates from the 1950s and features P.J. Edwards' tobacconist and confectioners shop at No. 30 High Street.

A closer view of P.J. Edwards' window display. The shop is now a modern fashion shop called Bling-Bling.

Opposite: Steam trams proved rather unpopular due to the noise and smell associated with them. They were eventually replaced by electric trams in 1907, an event commemorated on this postcard.

1906

PAST AND PRESENT

1907

A postcard showing Frederick Green's corn and seed merchants at No. 33 High Street on the corner of Springfield Drive opposite Station Road. At No. 37 was Robert Hayward's furniture dealers (now a new Kentucky Fried Chicken outlet). This postcard dates from the time of the steam trams in 1906.

This picture dates from after 1907 as it clearly shows an electric tram. J.K. Bourne's corn merchants took over Green's shop in 1915. By the 1960s it had become Proffitt and Westwood's seed shop. Note the newly planted trees lining the roadside. In the distance on the right, a row of lamps can be seen hanging outside Taylor's grocers.

Cecil Cariss had originally been based opposite Woolworth's in the early 1900s. By the 1950s, it had occupied the first floor of this building on the corner of Station Road. The ground floor was occupied by Brown & Clark plumber's merchants.

Station Road to Valentine Road

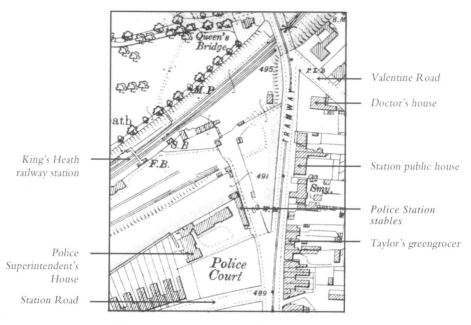

King's Heath railway station

Police Superintendent's House

Station Road

Valentine Road

Doctor's house

Station public house

Police Station stables

Taylor's greengrocer

Above: Station Road to Valentine Road, earlier map.

Below: Station Road to Valentine Road, later map.

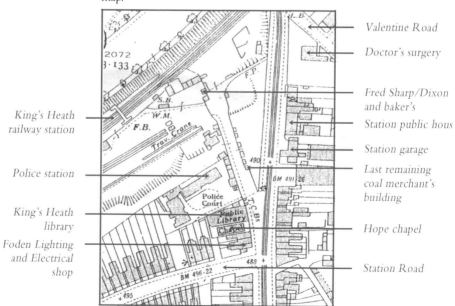

King's Heath railway station

Police station

King's Heath library

Foden Lighting and Electrical shop

Valentine Road

Doctor's surgery

Fred Sharp/Dixon and baker's

Station public hous

Station garage

Last remaining coal merchant's building

Hope chapel

Station Road

Above: The picture above shows the corner of Station Road with Foden's 'lighting & electrical' store. Foden's was based in this shop from the 1960s until the 1990s. The shop is now selling school uniforms.

Right: Hope Chapel next to King's Heath Library.

Above and below: Hope Chapel was situated on what is now the site of the children's library extension next to King's Heath Library. The site was originally used by the Seventh Day Adventist church from 1913, but by the 1930s it had become Hope Chapel. The original chapel was set back from the road. A small fence with iron railings ran between the library and Edith Fischer's photography shop at No. 2 High Street. Access was via a small iron gate in the middle of the fence. One would then walk through a small garden in front of the old building. Hope Chapel was knocked down in 1984.

Above and below: King's Heath Library was built in 1905. When the building was being constructed, a letter was received from the police station next door questioning the nuisance of smoke from the chimneys and the obstruction of the view from the superintendent's house. In March 1906 Mr William Skelton was appointed as the town's first librarian. Mr West was appointed as senior library assistant and Mr W. Seeley as junior assistant. The library was officially opened on 11 June 1906. At the opening ceremony the architect, Mr A. Gilbey Latham, presented Councillor E.A. Olivieri (chairman of the free libraries committee) with a gold key. This was used to officially open the iron front gates for the first time.

The front of the library in 1987. The stone used to face the building was a type of sandstone called Hollington stone.

The new children's library extension, built in 1984 on the site of Hope Chapel.

Above and below: The old Victorian police station next to the library was built in the 1880s and '90s. The first building on the left was originally the superintendent's house; the view from here was obstructed by the new library. At the time John Chare was the superintendent. The station originally had stables for police horses and its own well. However, all but one part of the original structure was demolished when the station was modernised in 1996.

This page: These pictures show King's Heath's special police in the 1920s. Both groups were photographed in the playground of the boarding school.

Opposite above: This picture shows the King's Heath police force in front of the superintendent's house in 1906. At this time King's Heath police were part of Worcestershire Constabulary and the officers are wearing the uniform of this county.

Opposite below: Another image of King's Heath police in 1906, but this time in the new style of Worcestershire Constabulary uniform, complete with helmets.

Above is Thomas Taylor's grocery and provision shop at No. 21 High Street opposite the police station. His shop is listed there from the late 1890s until the 1960s. By the 1930s his shop was occupying Nos 21 and 23 High Street.

Nos 17 and 19 High Street in 1988. They are now the only two remaining of a row of old shops. The tailor Phillip Collier was originally based at No. 19 (the right-hand shop). They later purchased Taylor's shop next door. They had it demolished and their new shop now occupies Nos 21-23 High Street. It is just visible at the far right of the picture.

Postcard showing the premises of coal merchants William Baker & Son at King's Heath railway station. William Baker is the man with the beard and standing directly in front of him is his son. The building in the background is the Station pub. The huge sign on its roof advertises 'Kendrick's home brewed ales'.

The entrance drive to the station was eventually lined with coal merchants' sheds, as seen in these images. William Baker merged with Mr T.H. Dixon and moved to different premises, pictured here. The small white gate and fence to the right of his premises mark the pedestrian footpath leading up towards the High Street through another gate opposite Dr Graham Young's house at No. 1 High Street on the corner of Valentine Road, seen in the background. This picture dates from 1910.

William Baker in a slightly more formal photograph with his family. He died at his residence in Woodville Road aged eighty-two years. He was clerk of All Saints church from May 1866.

William Baker and Mr Dixon sold out to Fred Sharp in the 1920s. Their old premises are pictured here after the takeover. However, the small wooden plaque by the window still says 'Dixon & Baker'. The man in the doorway is Leslie Williams. The pedestrian footpath to the right of the building can be seen more easily in this image.

Photograph showing the line of the pedestrian path with its fence from the High Street towards the station, still present as late as 1977.

A remarkable image showing the survival of one of the old coal merchants' buildings in 1988. It was eventually demolished in 1989. One can clearly recognise the modern structure of Windsor House on the High Street in the background.

Above and below: These two old postcards show King's Heath railway station looking towards Moseley in the 1900s. The original station opened in 1841 and was named, rather confusingly, Moseley station. It was finally called King's Heath station in 1867. The postcards show the up-line (i.e. towards Moseley) buildings on the left. In the distance one can make out the footbridge and the road bridge that carries the High Street over the railway line. It was named in honour of Queen Victoria's accession to the throne just before the railway was built; it is called Queen's Bridge.

Above and below: These two photographs date from 1966 and show the abandoned down-line station buildings. King's Heath station closed to passengers in January 1941. The station remained open to goods traffic until May 1966, when it closed to all traffic. One picture shows the buildings on the High Street in the background (left) and the old police station building (to the right).

These two photographs from the 1980s and '90s show the Station public house at No. 7 High Street. It was built by William and Elizabeth Frost in 1889, although it is Elizabeth who is listed as the owner. She remained at the pub until 1897.

The building to the right of the pub was originally Joshua Kent's garage at No. 9A High Street and later became known as the Station Garage.

No. 1 High Street in the 1970s. The house dates back to the late 1800s and has been the residence of many King's Heath doctors. In the 1920s and '30s it was Dr Graham Young's surgery. By the 1960s it was Dr Laurence Hodgson's practice.

Eventually in the 1980s the house became empty. It was then occupied by the Kinmos (King's Heath and Moseley) Charity. They provide a centre to support local people who suffer from mental health problems.

The End of the Journey

Well, we have arrived safely at Queen's Bridge and we could carry on up the hill towards Moseley Village but there is a lot more to King's Heath than just the High Street. There are many more streets, roads, farms, parks, businesses, people and places to be covered in the future. So here is a taster of things to come...

King's Heath has had a number of famous and not-so-famous residents over the years; the writers Barbara Cartland and J.R.R. Tolkien spent time in King's Heath and between them they have sold billions of books all over the world. Less well-known today are Edward Davison of Midland Wire Cordage Co., whose company fitted lightning conductors to a number of buildings in King's Heath including All Saints church, and Anthony Pratt, inventor of the game Cluedo, who lived on Stanley Road. We also have our near neighbours living on the other side of the railway line: Richard Cadbury at Uffculme and Joseph, Neville and Austen Chamberlain at Highbury. But let's not forget the singer and actress Toyah Willcox – a local girl whose father built many houses in King's Heath.

King's Heath has seen many changes over the years, like the coming of the steam tram, then the electric tram and now the buses that plough up and down the High Street. Will the tram return in the future? Also, changes in technology like the rise and fall of the typewriter; it's less than twenty years since the Typewriter Centre closed down, brought about by the rise of the personal computer. The change in the usage of local shops and the rise of supermarkets have changed the face of the High Street but if you look above the shop windows on some of the older buildings you can still see what they were like many years ago.

If you have read this book and think you may have some material or photographs of King's Heath that you would like to share with future generations please contact King's Heath Library where, with your permission, we can copy or scan them. The address is:

King's Heath Library
High Street
King's Heath
Birmingham
B14 7SW

Telephone: 0121 464 1515
Email: kings.heath.library@birmingham.gov.uk

One thing that this book has shown is the importance of recording changes in an area because what may not appear to be important today will be history in the future and the age of the local postcard is over. So we must thank Stan Budd for recording many of these changes over the years and remember that history is yesterday.

"Highbury"
r Chamberlain's Residence

A postcard showing Highbury, the home of Joseph Chamberlain. It was built in 1878 and designed by John Henry Chamberlain, who was no relation to Joseph. By 1915 it was being used as a hospital for wounded soldiers from the First World War.

Uffculme - From South East.

Uffculme has the date 1890 carved above its entrance and the initials of Richard Cadbury, for whom the house was built. It was used to house Belgian refugees in 1914 and by 1916 had been converted to a hospital for injured soldiers with over 200 beds.

The Priory in Vicarage Road: home of the Cartland family from the 1850s until 1940. The house was occupied by John Cartland until his death in 1896 and then by his eldest son John Howard Cartland. Prolific novelist Barbara Cartland was a relative and visited the Priory many times. It was demolished and Camp Hill School now stands in its grounds.

A nearly deserted Vicarage Road at its junction with Abbots Road looking towards the High Street. Until the 1870s, when the vicarage of All Saints church was built, it was called Black Lane, Bleak Lane or Blake Lane.

The photograph above shows Ashfield Road, the first home of the author J.R.R. Tolkien. He was born in Bloemfontein, South Africa on 3 January 1892. Tolkien came to England in the spring of 1895 with his mother Mabel and his younger brother Hilary. His father Arthur Tolkien died in February 1896. That summer, Mabel and the boys rented a cottage in the small hamlet of Sarehole near Birmingham. In 1901 Mabel and the boys returned to King's Heath and rented a house in Westfield Road.

The original St Dunstan's Catholic church, situated on the corner of Westfield Road and Station Road. This was where the Tolkien family worshipped.

Above and below: King's Heath Park is actually the grounds and garden of King's Heath House (see below). The house was built in 1832 for the newly elected MP William Congreve Russell. He later became both a Deputy Lieutenant and High Sheriff of Worcestershire. He left the house in 1835. In 1880 the house was bought from the Ingleby family by John Cartland. On 9 November 1908 the house and the surrounding land was purchased by the Kings Norton and Northfield Urban District Council for £11,000. The council responded to popular demand and immediately opened the grounds as a public park. The house, known locally as the White House, is currently a school of horticulture.